AWESOME OCEANS
ANIMALS OF THE
ICY SEAS

Michael Bright

Copper Beech Books
Brookfield, Connecticut

© Aladdin Books Ltd 2002

Produced by:
Aladdin Books Ltd
28 Percy Street
London W1T 2BZ

ISBN 0-7613-2750-9

*First published in the
United States in 2002 by:*
Copper Beech Books,
an imprint of
The Millbrook Press
2 Old New Milford Road
Brookfield, Connecticut 06804

Editor:
Kathy Gemmell

Designers:
Flick, Book Design & Graphics
Simon Morse

Illustrators:
James Field, Terry Riley, Chris
Tomlin, Ross Watton—SGA,
Ray Coombs, Darren Harvey,
Karen Johnson, Michael J. Loatea,
Richard Orr, Justine Peek,
John Rignall, Mike Saunders,
Chris Shields, Stephen Sweet,
Ian Thompson, Norman Weaver
Cartoons: Jo Moore

Certain illustrations have
appeared in earlier books
created by Aladdin Books.

Printed in U.A.E.

Cataloging-in-Publication
data is on file at the
Library of Congress.

Contents

Introduction

Polar seas are places of great extremes. With wild waves, subzero temperatures, and vast stretches of pack ice, the Arctic Ocean and the Antarctic's Southern Ocean are two of the most terrible places on Earth. Yet, millions of animals arrive from all over the world to breed or feed here, for in summer there is food—plenty of it. Tiny plants and animals called plankton flourish, providing plentiful food for fish, birds, and mammals. Some of the world's biggest animals and fiercest predators live in these inhospitable waters.

Spot and count!

Q: Why watch for these boxes?

A: For answers to the animal questions you always wanted to ask.

zoom in on...

Bits and pieces

These boxes take a closer look at features of certain animals or places.

Awesome facts

Watch for these puffin diamonds to learn more weird and wonderful facts about the animals of the icy seas and their freezing world.

Polar seas

Polar seas are dominated by ice. The ice changes in surface area, shrinking in summer and expanding in winter. It forms in the fall when the winds drop and the surface is still. As the temperature dips below freezing, the sea first becomes a soup of ice crystals, then a layer like melted cheese, then finally an ice sheet, brittle like glass.

The Southern Ocean covers 10.8 million sq mi (28 m sq km) and surrounds Antarctica. In summer, only a small part of this is ice, but in winter, more than two-thirds of it has frozen. By midwinter, the sea ice may be 3 to 7 feet (1-2 m) thick.

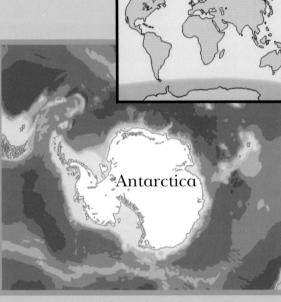

Southern Ocean

Antarctica

The Antarctic is home to many species of penguin, including the king penguin.

The coldest place on Earth so far recorded is Vostok, a Russian research station in the Antarctic, where the temperature once dropped to an incredible −128.6°F (−89.2°C) in winter.

Arctic Ocean

Canada
(North
America)

Arctic
Ocean
+

Russian
Federation
(Asia)

Three continents surround the Arctic Ocean—North America, Europe, and Asia. It is a small ocean, covering 5.6 million sq mi(14.5 m sq km). In summer, more than half of it is frozen. In winter, four-fifths is covered by ice.

Polar bears hunt on the Arctic ice.

Scandinavia
(Europe)

Q: Which is colder, the Arctic or the Antarctic?

A: The Antarctic is colder, but each has its own particular weather conditions. In the Antarctic, icy winds gust up to 140 miles per hour (225 km/h), but there is less snow than in the Arctic. At Ellesmere Island, in the Canadian Arctic, temperatures fall to –35.7°F (–37.6°C) in winter, but in some parts of the Antarctic they can go below –112°F (–80°C).

Finding food

There is little life in the center of the Arctic Ocean, but where it borders the warmer North Atlantic and Pacific Oceans, it is filled with nutrients. This is where Arctic animals live and feed. The Southern Ocean has strong surface currents that stir up nutrients from the depths, making them the richest waters for animal life in the world —richer even than the tropical seas.

? Q: Are both oceans the same?

A: No. The Arctic Ocean is generally much shallower. It is a basin with wide, shallow areas around the continent edges. The Southern Ocean has the continent of Antarctica in its center, which is weighed down by ice. At the edge of the continent, the land drops down steeply into a deep ocean plain.

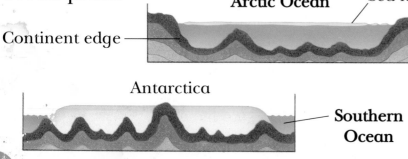

Arctic Ocean — Sea ice

Continent edge

Antarctica

Southern Ocean

Deadly killer whales hunt for food at both ends of the world. They live in pods and hunt together. This means that they can surround and attack large seals and whales as well as feeding on smaller prey.

Bull sperm whales head for polar waters in summer, when the food is plentiful. In the south, they swim close to Antarctica. In the north, they visit the zone between polar and warmer seas. They dive deep to catch giant squid, which can grow up to 60 feet (18 m) long.

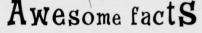

Awesome facts

Off the coast of Antarctica, the largest seals in the world, southern elephant seals, dive down more than a mile (2 km) to feed somewhere safe from killer whales.

Essential diet

The tiniest creatures in the sea are food for some of the biggest. Plankton and krill are near the bottom of the food chain, yet everything in the polar seas eats them. They are filtered out by giant baleen whales, scooped up by penguins and seals, and pecked at by seabirds. Without them, the oceans would be deserted.

Awesome facts
The total weight of krill in the sea is thought to be more than the weight of the entire human race on land— more than 700 million tons.

Plankton are tiny, drifting plants and animals found at the surface of the sea. Phytoplankton (right) is the "plant" variety of plankton, which uses energy from the sun to produce food. During the 24 hours of daylight in polar summers, it blooms to form a thick soup at the surface of the water. It also grows in dimples on the underside of the ice, where it is grazed on by krill and small fish.

zoom in on...

Bubble netting

A humpback whale can catch huge quantities of krill by surrounding them with a net of bubbles blown underwater from its blowhole. The krill are frightened into a tight ball by the shiny bubbles. All the whale has to do then is swim up through the trap with its mouth open. It filters out the sea water through narrow plates of bone, called baleen, hanging from the roof of its mouth, so that just the krill are left behind in its mouth.

Krill are plankton-eating, shrimplike crustaceans, between $1/2$ inch (1 cm) and 6 inches (15 cm) long. A swarm of krill in the Southern Ocean can cover up to 175 sq mi (450 sq km). They swim forward with five pairs of paddle-like legs and can go backward for short bursts using their tails. They must swim constantly—if they stop, they sink.

Q: Why don't fish in the Antarctic freeze?

A: Many Antarctic fish survive at water temperatures in which they should freeze solid, but they don't. Their blood contains antifreeze chemicals, similar to those put into car radiators in winter. This stops their blood and tissues from freezing.

Can you spot three other ice fish in the main picture?

zoom in on...

Overfishing

Stocks of cod in the North Atlantic and fringes of the Arctic Ocean are dropping alarmingly, so fishing fleets are turning to the Southern Ocean. Now, not only fish are being targeted, but also swarms of krill, the essential part of most food chains in the Antarctic.

Ice fish

There are some weird fish in polar seas. All have adapted to the icy conditions. In the south, most fish lurk in the depths. The Antarctic plunder fish, for example, guards its eggs on the sea bed, far under the ice. In the north, dense shoals of Arctic cod, char, herring, and capelin feast on the summer blooms of plankton in surface waters.

The ghostly, 2 $\frac{1}{2}$-foot (75-cm)-long Antarctic ice fish is a bottom-dweller. It looks pale because its blood has few red blood cells in it. Because these carry oxygen around the body, the heart of the ice fish is twice the expected size because it must pump ten times harder to supply its body with enough oxygen.

Penguins

The Southern Ocean is teeming with penguins. They cannot fly, and they walk with a comical waddle, but they are superb swimmers. Most eat krill, but larger species eat squid or fish. All must return to land to breed. Near mainland Antarctica, they are mostly Adélie penguins.

Q: Are there penguins in the Arctic?

A: No. But there are penguinlike birds called auks. These swim like penguins but can also fly. The biggest was a flightless auk, the great auk, that looked and behaved very much like a penguin. It was killed for its fat, feathers, and eggs and became extinct in 1844.

Penguins "fly" through the water using their flippers. In a one-week fishing trip, a king penguin (above) will make up to 1,200 dives and cover an area of 164 sq mi (424 sq km). However, only about one dive in ten results in catching any fish or squid.

The emperor penguin is the largest penguin. The male spends the bitter winter on the ice, with an egg and then the newly hatched chick balanced on its feet, tucked under a protective fold of thick skin and feathers. The males huddle together to keep out the cold until their partners return from the sea to take over nursery duties.

Awesome facts
Zavodovski Island, an active volcano in the Southern Ocean, has the largest penguin colony on Earth: a noisy 2 million chinstrap and macaroni penguins.

If a chinstrap penguin chick is left for a second, a skua will grab it right from under its mother's sharp bill. The skua has chicks too, and it nests at the same time to ensure a good supply of penguin food.

Sheathbills eat penguin eggs and small chicks. They will even grab food being passed from parent to chick. In hard times, sheathbills feed on penguin droppings, seaweed, and small animals that live in the seaweed.

14

Attack from the air

In the middle of vast breeding colonies, away from the sea, penguins have little defense from the savage bills of predatory and scavenging birds. Skuas, petrels, and sheathbills often nest close to colonies, where the great numbers and extreme weather mean that there are always plenty of penguins to eat, dead or alive.

How many skuas are there in this picture?

zoom in on...

Petrel's bill

Giant petrels are the vultures of the Southern Ocean. They have huge nostrils on top of the bill and can smell as well as see food from some distance away. They are both scavengers and predators, eating seal carcasses and young penguins with equal gusto.

Nostrils

15

Huge rafts of blue-eyed cormorants sit on the sea's surface and feed together. Every so often, a bird glances below the surface looking for a fish shoal. If it spots one, it dives and the rest of the flock follows. In the confusion, fish almost jump into the cormorants' mouths.

The wandering albatross migrates huge distances around the Southern Ocean. It glides effortlessly in search of squid or fish, buoyed up by air currents created by waves. When it returns to its nest, it regurgitates (brings up) the food for its giant fluffy chicks. Unlike many birds, partners stay together for life.

Awesome facts

A wandering albatross with a wingspan of a massive 12 feet (3.63 m) has been documented, but some may have a wingspan of up to 16 feet (5 m).

Soaring and diving

Southern Ocean seabirds have adopted many different techniques for catching food. Wandering albatrosses have the greatest wingspan of any bird and can soar over miles of sea in search of concentrations of squid. Wilson's storm petrels flit over the surface and pick off krill and other small creatures. Terns make shallow dives to catch small fish just under the water.

Lamellae

zoom in on...

Filter feeding

The broad-billed prion moves across the sea's surface, wings outstretched, head underwater, and feet propelling it forward. It filters out food particles using its special bill, fringed with tiny projections called lamellae. These are similar to the baleen plates of the great whales (see page 9). With this system it can filter an incredible 40,000 plankton in each feeding session.

Polar bears

Polar bears live mainly on the Arctic pack ice, moving south in winter as the ice extends and north in summer when it melts back. Their white fur camouflages them on the ice, helping them stalk prey without being seen. Under the fur, their black skin absorbs heat. Hollow hairs and a thick layer of blubber (fat) also keep out the cold.

zoom in on...

Scavenging

Each fall, polar bears arrive at the town of Churchill, on the edge of Hudson Bay. They have spent summer in the forest, but hunt on the ice in winter. If the ice is late in forming, they hang around the dump. They sometimes enter the town and make a nuisance of themselves.

Q: Can polar bears swim?

A: Yes! Despite their "dog paddle" swimming style, polar bears are fantastic swimmers. They are true marine mammals and can swim many miles from one ice floe to another. To help them to do this, their coat is water repellent and their feet are partly webbed.

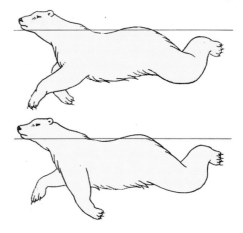

A female polar bear gives birth, usually to twins, in a snow den in winter. After eating little all winter, she is hungry and must hunt seals to put on weight and produce milk for her cubs. But she must be careful. If a male bear spots them, he will attack the mother and kill the cubs.

Awesome facts

When stalking seals on the ice, a polar bear was once seen to cover up its black nose with its furry paw so that it could not be seen!

On the ice

Seals are mammals. They get oxygen from the air, so they must return to the surface regularly to breathe. In the spring, they leave the water to pup (give birth) in snow or ice dens or on top of the ice itself. When out of the water, Arctic seals are in danger of being eaten by the region's number one killer—the polar bear.

How many male hooded seals can you count?

Hooded seals live in the Arctic. At breeding time the males display to females and to one another. They do this by blowing out the lining of one nostril into an outsize red balloon, or by inflating their black nose hood.

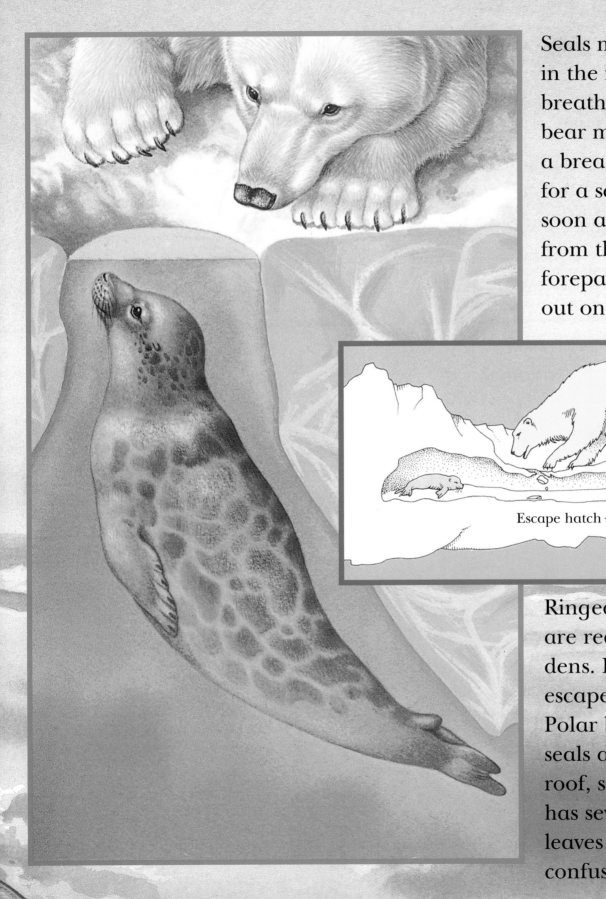

Seals maintain open holes in the ice so that they can breathe regularly. A polar bear may sit for hours at a breathing hole, waiting for a seal to surface. As soon as it does, one swipe from the bear's powerful forepaw will haul the seal out onto the ice.

Escape hatch

Ringed seal pups are reared in snow dens. Each den has an escape hatch to the sea. Polar bears can smell the seals and break in the roof, so a mother often has several dens. She leaves some empty to confuse the bears.

21

zoom in on...

Walrus

In summer, hundreds of male walrus haul themselves out onto Round Island, Alaska, to sun themselves. When they leave the water they are pale grey. This is because the blood withdraws from their skin in cold water so that they don't lose heat. As they warm up, the blood reaches their skin and they turn bright pink.

The leopard seal is one of the Antarctic's fiercest marine predators. It stakes out penguin colonies and grabs the birds when they enter the water. It throws its victim into the air and skins it alive before swallowing the flesh.

The Weddell seal patrols an under-ice territory, which it defends by making a singing noise. It has a breathing hole that it must keep clear, using its teeth to chisel away regularly at the ice. Eventually, its teeth wear down or rot and the seal dies because it cannot keep its ice hole open.

Seal patrols

Seals appeared in the northern hemisphere about 30 million years ago. During a cold period in the Earth's history, some headed south. Today, the crabeater seal population in the Antarctic is the largest in the world—possibly more than 15 million seals—making it the most numerous large mammal on the planet after humans.

Icy whales

Many species of whale live permanently in or visit polar seas. Blue whales spend the summer gulping down krill in Antarctic waters. In the Arctic, bowhead whales skim the ocean for sea butterflies. Minke whales let seabirds guide them to shoals of fish at the surface in both the Arctic and Antarctic.

After blue whales, fin whales (below) are the largest animals in the sea. With their powerful muscles and streamlined shape, they are the fastest of the big whales. They migrate to the polar seas each summer to feed.

24

Q: Why does the narwhal have a horn?

A: It's not a horn. The Arctic narwhal's peculiar spear is a long, spiral tooth, or tusk, that erupts from its upper lip. It is used to joust with other males in competitions for females. Females do not have a tusk.

White whales, or belugas, live in the Arctic. They were known to ancient mariners as sea canaries because they sing and chirp so much. They swim to river estuaries in summer to molt and give birth to pups. Here the water is slightly warmer than in the icy sea.

Count how many legs the decolopoda (giant sea spider) has.

The giant sea spider is not a true spider. (A true spider has eight legs.) Although it is the size of a human palm, its body is tiny, so some of its internal organs are squeezed into its ten spindly legs. It feeds by sucking out the juices from other invertebrates.

zoom in on...

Amphipods

Amphipods are crustaceans. The largest amphipod in the Antarctic is an amazing 35 inches (90 cm) long—five times larger than its tropical cousin. Animals grow huge in cold seas because there is more oxygen there. They grow in bursts when food is plentiful.

Under the ice

Even under the ice, life can be as colorful as on any tropical reef. There is a greater diversity of species in the Antarctic than the Arctic. Animals grow more slowly, live longer, and grow bigger in these bitterly cold conditions. The Antarctic waters are home to invertebrate giants like amphipods—some of which live for 100 years or more.

The Greenland sleeper shark of the Arctic grows up to 21 feet (6.5 m) long. It has small, glowing creatures called copepods attached to its eyes. These are thought to lure prey, such as small fish, into the shark's mouth. It catches fish and squid and scavenges on the carcasses of drowned caribou or dead seals.

Q: How do icebergs form?

A: They calve (break off) from glaciers and ice shelves and float on the sea's surface. Only one third can be seen above the water, and the rest is hidden below the surface. Some icebergs can be several miles wide. Ocean currents carry them toward warmer seas, where they eventually melt. Fish and krill gather underneath the icebergs, and seals and penguins hitch a ride on top.

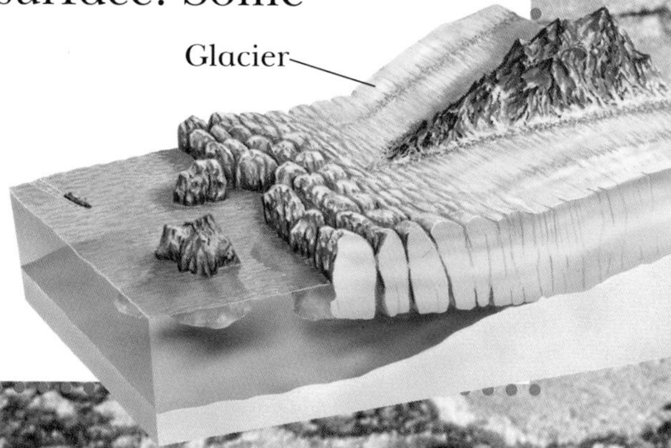

Glacier

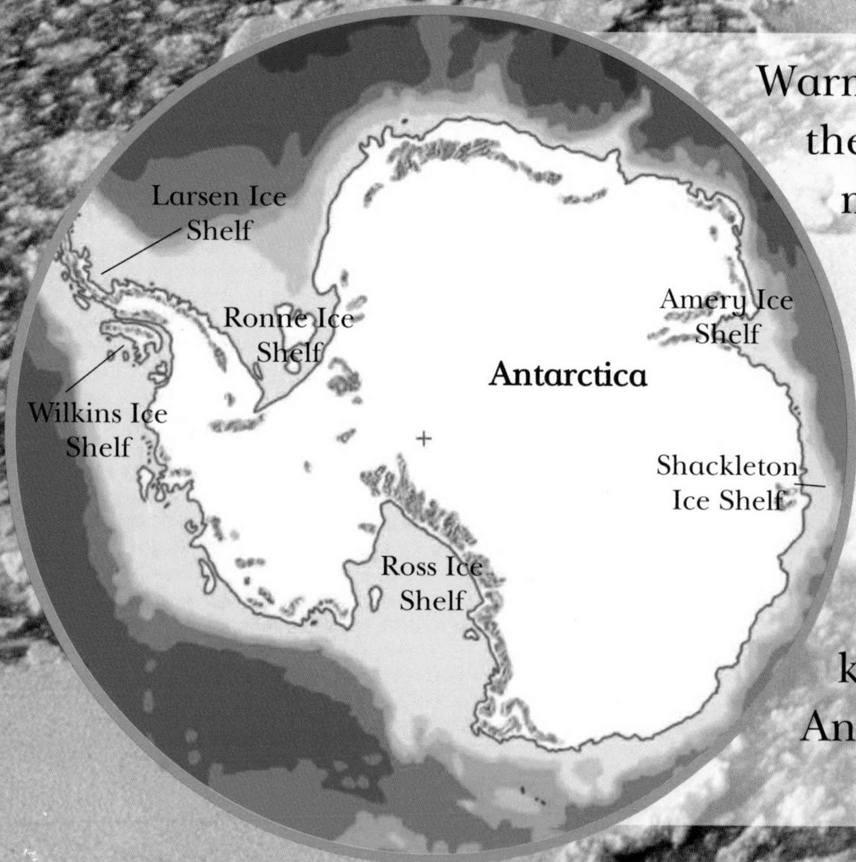

Larsen Ice Shelf

Ronne Ice Shelf

Wilkins Ice Shelf

Amery Ice Shelf

Antarctica

Shackleton Ice Shelf

Ross Ice Shelf

Warmer temperatures are causing the Antarctic ice shelves to melt. During the summer of 1998-99, the Larsen and Wilkins Ice Shelves alone lost more than 1,100 sq mi (3,000 sq km) of ice. Scientists estimate that in the 50 years before that, only 2,700 sq mi (7,000 sq km) were lost from all the Antarctic ice shelves together.

A hole in the Earth's ozone layer over the Antarctic enlarges considerably in the summer months (in white, left). This allows more harmful ultraviolet rays from the sun to reach the Earth's surface, and this is dangerous to people and wildlife.

How many tourists can you count on the Antarctic ice breaker below?

Warming up

The polar regions have warmed up during the last few decades, largely due to polluting gases—mainly the "greenhouse gas" carbon dioxide (CO_2)—that escape from cars, factories, and homes. In the Arctic, the average annual temperature is up by 1.8°F (1°C) and in the Antarctic by 4.5°F (2.5°C) since the 1940s. This is double the warming in the rest of the world, and the polar ice is melting.

Icy seas in danger

Polar regions are under threat. Antarctic species are in danger because their main food, krill, is being fished commercially. Overfishing threatens to undermine food chains throughout the Southern Ocean—every creature, from blue whales to tiny Wilson's storm petrels, would be affected.

Large-scale commercial whaling ceased in 1986, but whale stocks in the Antarctic, such as those of the blue whale, have been slow to recover. Yet some nations continue to catch whales, such as minke whales in the Southern Ocean, supposedly for scientific purposes. The meat, however, is sold commercially.

zoom in on...

Toxic Arctic

Pollution is blown into the Arctic Ocean from far away, so that even in the remotest parts of the Arctic, animals such as polar bears and belugas are contaminated. Oil prospecting is also a threat, as oil spills could melt the ice and pollute the sea.

Glossary

blubber
The thick layer of fat under the skin of whales and seals that keeps them warm in the bitter cold.

camouflage
The way in which an animal hides from predators or stalks prey by blending in with its surroundings.

crustacean
A hard-bodied animal without a backbone but with numerous hanging body parts that have a variety of functions, from eating to walking.

diversity
The richness and variety of species in a particular area.

food chain
The transfer of food and energy from plants through small animals that eat them, to larger animals that eat the small animals.

glacier
A "river" of ice that spills into the sea or a lake.

"greenhouse gas"
One of certain gases that build up in the Earth's atmosphere and trap heat from the sun near the planet's surface, causing the Earth to warm up.

ice shelf
A wide strip of ice, which is attached to the land but floats in the sea.

invertebrate
An animal with no backbone.

mammals
A backboned animal with hair, such as a bear, which feeds its young on milk.

migration
The movement of animals to and from particular parts of the world, such as feeding and breeding grounds.

molt
The ability of an animal to lose old skin, fur, or feathers and replace them with new.

nutrient
Any nourishing foodstuff.

ozone layer
One of the layers in the atmosphere that protects the Earth from dangerous ultraviolet rays from the sun.

pack ice
Ice floating on the sea, which freezes in winter and melts in summer.

pollution
Substances that can damage the environment, such as waste and chemicals.

predator
An animal that hunts and eats other animals.

prey
An animal that is hunted and eaten by other animals.

scavenger
An animal that eats dead animals, often those that have been killed by predators.

species
Animals that resemble one another closely and are able to breed together.

31

Index